Benjamin Franklin

Wendy Conklin, M.A.

Table of Contents

Just a Printer?

Benjamin Franklin wrote his own **epitaph** (EP-uh-taf) when he was only 22 years old. He wanted the top of his tombstone to read: *B. Franklin, Printer.* Was this Franklin's greatest role? He must have thought so. He never changed his epitaph. It is true that he was a gifted writer and printer. But many agree that his other gifts were more important than this one.

The self-written ▶ epitaph of Franklin

Benjamin Franklin

◀ Franklin as a boy working in his brother's printing shop

His Early Years

Benjamin Franklin was born in Boston on January 17, 1706. He taught himself to read the Bible when he was just five years old.

His father hoped he would become a preacher, but this was not a good fit for Franklin. More than anything Franklin wanted to be a sailor. His father said, "No way!"

Franklin's brother James had his own newspaper. Franklin became James's **apprentice** (uh-PREN-tis) when he was 12 years old. This was how he became a printer.

Boston Gazette from 1721 printed by James Franklin ▶

◀ **Franklin working as an apprentice**

Becoming a Printer

James Franklin received letters signed by Mrs. Silence Dogood. He printed the letters in his newspaper. No one knew who Mrs. Dogood was. She made fun of the latest fashions and social events. Her letters made the newspaper very popular. Little did people know that it was Benjamin Franklin who was actually writing these letters.

Ten years later, Franklin started his own printing business. He was probably best known for his book *Poor Richard's Almanack*. **Almanacs** (OL-muh-naks) were printed yearly. Each year, the almanac predicted the weather. It also told about the special city events planned for the year.

▼ **Title page of the 1748** *Poor Richard's Almanack*

Franklin's printing press ▶

Poor Mr. Leed

A man named Mr. Leed had the most popular almanac in town. Franklin decided to play a joke on Mr. Leed. Franklin wanted his almanac to be more popular. So, Franklin predicted that Leed wouldn't be able to print his almanac anymore because he was going to die soon. When Leed's almanac came out the following year, Franklin wrote that Leed's ghost had printed it. This joking continued back and forth for years.

Franklin, as a ▶
young man,
in front of his
print shop

To Parliament for the Stamp Tax

Benjamin Franklin became very popular in Philadelphia. He was so popular that Pennsylvania chose him to speak for them in Britain's **Parliament** (PAR-luh-muhnt).

Parliament signed the Stamp Tax when Franklin was in London. Franklin had been away from the colonies for too long. He did not think that the colonists would mind this tax. He even made some of his friends stamp agents to collect the tax. The colonists said, "Franklin is a traitor!"

When Franklin saw how upset the colonists were, he got to work right away. In less than a year, he helped get the tax **repealed** (ri-PEELD).

▲ Colonial soldiers arresting Franklin's son

Royal Governor

Franklin helped his son William get a job as the governor of New Jersey. Later, Benjamin regretted doing this. His son sided with the king during the Revolutionary War.

◀ A Stamp Act official being beaten by angry citizens

The Hutchinson Letters

Franklin did not like the way England treated the colonists. A member of Parliament told Franklin to stop complaining. This man said that the colonists wanted it that way. He gave Franklin a packet of letters to prove this.

The letters were written by Thomas Hutchinson. Hutchinson was the governor of Massachusetts. The letters asked the king to punish the **Patriots** (PAY-tree-uhtz). Patriots were the colonists who wanted to break free from England. Franklin was shocked that a colonial leader wrote such things.

Map of Massachusetts ▶ where Hutchinson was governor

Governor
Thomas Hutchinson

Franklin sent the letters to a friend in Massachusetts. Franklin told his friend not to show the letters to anyone. But Franklin knew this man would not keep the secret. Before long the letters were passed around for everyone to see. The letters were very upsetting. People felt that Hutchinson had betrayed them.

▼ A duel from the time period

▲ Dueling pistol

Dueling Over Letters

The Hutchinson letters caused a duel between two men in England. One blamed the other for stealing the letters. When Franklin heard about it, he admitted he had sent the letters to the colonies.

▲ Benjamin Franklin representing colonial interests in London

A Popular Diplomat

Franklin was a great **diplomat**. He did his best to represent Pennsylvania while he was in England. Massachusetts, Georgia, and New Jersey chose him to represent him in front of the king as well.

Franklin did not want the colonies to break away from England. Instead, he hoped that both sides could work out their problems.

Meanwhile, the First **Continental** (kon-tuh-NEN-tuhl) **Congress** met in Philadelphia. They wrote a letter called the Declaration of Rights and Grievances (GREE-vuhn-zez). Since Franklin was their diplomat, they sent the letter to him. Franklin delivered the letter to the king.

To the Second Continental Congress

When Franklin arrived home, Pennsylvania had an election. They chose him to be their delegate to the Second Continental Congress.

Over time, Franklin changed his mind about war. He realized that war was the only solution to the problems. He left England in 1775. He wanted to return home to prepare for war.

Declaration of Rights and Grievances ▼

13

Franklin and Jefferson on the Declaration

Franklin worked on a committee with Thomas Jefferson. They were in charge of writing a **document**. It told the world that the colonies did not want to be ruled by the British king. It was called the Declaration of Independence.

Jefferson did most of the writing for the document. Franklin and the committee changed only a few lines.

The Declaration of Independence committee: Roger Sherman,
▼ Thomas Jefferson, Benjamin Franklin, John Adams, and Robert Livingston

Then, they shared the document with Congress. Congress debated it line by line.

It was hard for Jefferson to hear others criticize (KRIT-uh-size) his work. He sat next to Franklin during the meetings. Franklin tried to make Jefferson feel better.

Signing the Declaration

The signers of the Declaration of Independence were called traitors by Great Britain. But, these men weren't afraid. John Hancock signed the document first and made his signature extra large. Franklin added extra lines below his name to make it stand out.

Thomas Jefferson

▼ Congress signs the Declaration of Independence

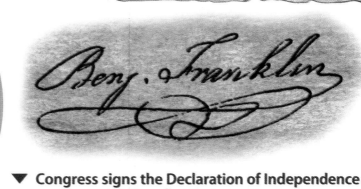

A Trip to France

Congress knew they needed help if they were to win the war. They sent Franklin to France to ask for both money and soldiers.

The French did not want to fight a losing battle. After a year of waiting, the French agreed to help. Franklin's hard work had paid off.

Benjamin Franklin

Franklin's ▶ first meeting with the king of France

Franklin was asked to meet with the French king. There were certain rules to follow when meeting the king. One rule was that men had to wear wigs. Franklin tried to find a wig to wear at the **ceremony** (SER-uh-mo-nee). His head was just too big and no one could find a wig that fit. So, Franklin went bareheaded. The king was impressed. He thought Franklin's choice not to wear a wig was a **symbol** of freedom.

Trying on Wigs

When Franklin could not find a wig to fit, he said the wigs were too small. The wig makers replied that his head was just too big!

▼ Benjamin Franklin in France

▲ Benjamin Franklin returns to Philadelphia in 1785

Almost Home

At the end of the war, Franklin worked to **negotiate** (ni-GO-she-ate) peace with England. The **treaty** was written in France. This treaty stated that the colonies were free from England.

Franklin returned to America in 1785. He was upset to hear that the eagle had been chosen as America's symbol. He said that the eagle was dishonest and stole food from the hawk. He thought the turkey would have been a better choice!

Thomas Jefferson was made the new diplomat to France. A man asked Jefferson if he was replacing Franklin. Jefferson replied, "No one can *replace* him."

America's symbol, the Bald Eagle ▲

Thomas Jefferson

▼ Franklin working in Philadelphia

▼ Benjamin Franklin speaking at the Constitutional Convention

Creating the Constitution

Things in the United States were not going well. At 81 years old, Franklin helped remake the government. He met with other delegates in Philadelphia. They wrote the **Constitution** of the United States. At times, he was too weak to stand. So, he wrote his thoughts down and had others read them aloud.

Franklin was afraid that they would end up with a **monarchy** (MON-uhr-kee). So, he wanted more than just one president. And he did not want the presidents to receive pay. Delegates voted against these ideas. In the end, 40 men signed the new Constitution.

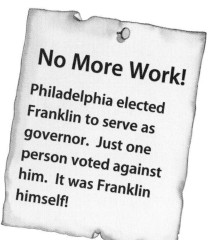

No More Work!

Philadelphia elected Franklin to serve as governor. Just one person voted against him. It was Franklin himself!

▼ Delegates signing the Constitution of the United States

21

The Death of a Great Man

Benjamin Franklin died on April 17, 1790. In his 1738 *Poor Richard's Almanack*, Franklin had written, "If you wou'd not be forgotten as soon as you are dead and rotten, either write things worth reading, or do things worth the writing."

Franklin truly fulfilled this statement. He was a great writer, and he was a great doer. He studied electricity, formed a library, and built a hospital. Franklin also began the first fire department and police force in Philadelphia. In so many ways he served his country well. Some say he was the greatest American to have ever lived.

▼ **Franklin's electricity experiment**

▲ **The Franklin Stove**

▼ **Print celebrating Franklin's long life**

▲ **An article written by Benjamin Franklin**

B. FRANKLIN, LL.D. F.R.S.

Born at Boston in New England, Jan. 6.ᵗʰ 1706.

Died at Philadelphia, April 17.ᵗʰ 1790.

Glossary

abolition—to get rid of, to do away with

almanacs—books that include a calendar, information on the movement of stars, and special days

apprentice—a person who learns a new trade

ceremony—a formal event

constitution—document that outlines the laws that govern a country

Continental Congress—meeting of delegates from the colonies to decide how to deal with Great Britain

delegate—person sent to represent and speak for a group

diplomat—a person who represents his or her country to another country

document—official government paper

epitaph—words written on a tombstone

monarchy—government ruled by a king or queen

negotiate—work with others to reach an agreement

Parliament—the British legislative branch that represents its people and makes its laws

Patriots—wanted freedom from British rule

repealed—thrown out, cancelled

symbol—something that represents the real thing

treaty—an agreement among countries